SEAS AND OCEANS

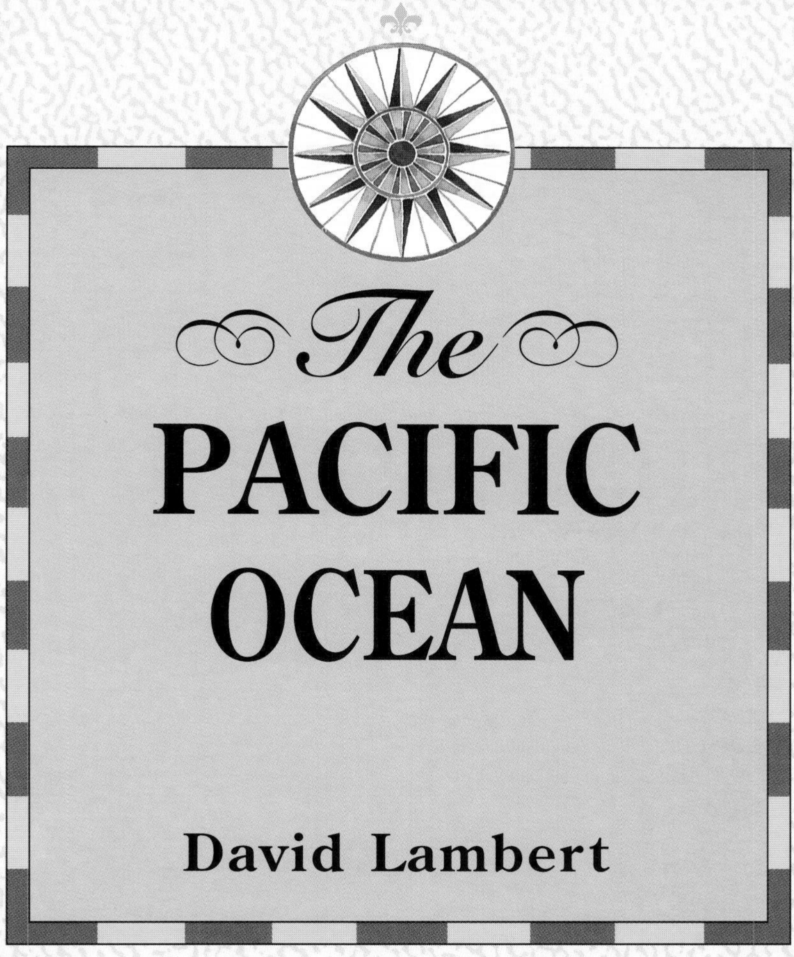

The PACIFIC OCEAN

David Lambert

RAINTREE STECK-VAUGHN PUBLISHERS
The Steck-Vaughn Company
Austin, Texas

Seas and Oceans series

The Atlantic Ocean
The Caribbean and the Gulf of Mexico
The Indian Ocean
The Mediterranean Sea
The North Sea and the Baltic Sea
The Pacific Ocean
The Polar Seas
The Red Sea and the Arabian Gulf

Cover: Moorea Island, Tahiti (© Superstock)

Published by Raintree Steck-Vaughn Publishers,
an imprint of Steck-Vaughn Company

Library of Congress Cataloging-in-Publication Data
Lambert, David.
The Pacific Ocean / David Lambert.
p. cm.—(Seas and oceans)
Includes bibliographical references and index.
Summary: Surveys the physical features, plant and animal life, human population, commerce, natural resources, and environmental concerns of the world's largest ocean.
ISBN 0-8172-4507-3
1. Pacific ocean—Juvenile literature.
[1. Pacific ocean.]
I. Title. II. Series: Seas and oceans (Austin, Tex.)
GC771.L36 1997
551.46'5—dc20 96-28228

Printed in Italy. Bound in the United States.
1 2 3 4 5 6 7 8 9 0 01 00 99 98 97

Picture acknowledgments:
Finn G. Anderson 10–11, Ecoscene 9 (Richard Glover), 15 (Sally Morgan), 23 (top/James Davis), 24–25 (Andy Hibbert), 45 (top/B. Kloske); Environmental Picture Library 30 (Marc Boettcher), 41 (U.S. Department of Energy); Eye Ubiquitous 17 (right/John Miles), 20 (Matthew McKee), 28 (Jim Holmes), 32–33 (Jim Holmes), 36 (Matthew McKee), 37 (James Davis), 43 (James Davis); Chris Fairclough 25 (top), 31; Frank Lane Picture Agency 33 (right/Silvestris), 40 (Mark Newman), 44–45 (Mark Newman); Geoscience 27; Nicky Gyopari 18–19 (both); Hulton Deutsch 26; Impact 10 (bottom/Tadashi Kajiyama), 35 (top/Philip Gordon), 38 (Ken Graham), 42–43 (Caroline Penn); Life File 8 (Jeremy Hoare), 22–23 (Sue Wheat), 39 (Emma Lee); Science Photo Library 7 (Dr. Ken Macdonald), 13 (bottom/NASA), 34–35 (David Parker); Tony Stone 4, 16–17 (Norbert Wu); All artwork is supplied by Hardlines except for Peter Bull 14 and Stephen Chabluk 12.

Contents

Words that appear in **bold** in the text can be found in the glossary on page 46.

INTRODUCTION

The Largest Ocean on Earth

The Pacific Ocean is easily the world's largest ocean. It covers more than one-third of our planet's surface—almost as much as all the other oceans combined. Every continent in the world could fit inside the Pacific, with space for an extra one as large as Asia left over.

The Pacific holds more water than all the other oceans put together. It has the greatest average depth, and in the Mariana Trench its floor plunges to the lowest place on Earth—almost seven miles below sea level.

This vast body of water lies east of Asia and Australia and west of the Americas. At its widest it stretches nearly halfway around the globe. From the cold Arctic in the north, the Pacific extends south through the tropics to frozen Antarctica.

Right: *This map of the Pacific region shows the ocean's fringing seas, main islands and island groups, and nations in and alongside the Pacific.*

Below: *The Great Barrier Reef is the world's largest, longest mass of coral. It stretches more than 1,250 miles along Australia's northeast coast.*

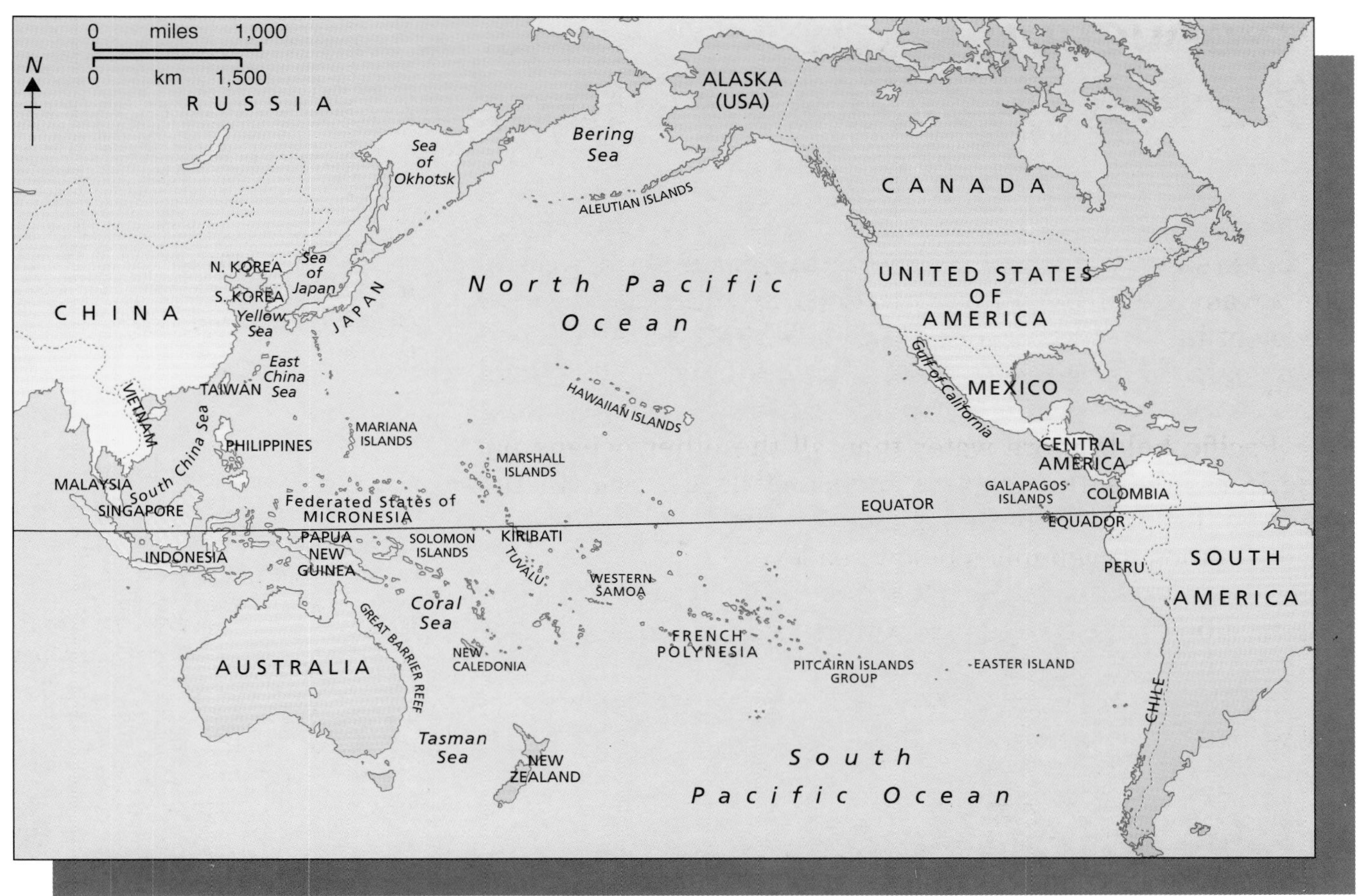

How big and how deep?	
Area	70 million sq. miles
Average water depth	14,000 feet
Maximum water depth	36,198 feet

The narrow Bering Strait between Asia and North America connects the Pacific with the Arctic Ocean to its north. In the south, wider sea areas south of Australia and South America link the Pacific with the Indian and Atlantic oceans.

Among the Pacific's most remarkable features is its large number of islands. Large islands or island groups include Japan, the Philippines, New Guinea, and New Zealand. But thousands of tiny islands also lie scattered across the western Pacific. Many of these are surrounded by low **coral reefs**. The Great Barrier Reef off northeast Australia is the world's largest coral reef. Islands in the west and north separate the Tasman Sea, Coral Sea, Sea of Japan, and other fringing seas from the rest of the Pacific Ocean. Although *pacific* means "calm," fierce winds and huge waves sometimes torment its surface. Yet Stone Age peoples in frail boats explored it. Today, cargo ships now regularly cross the Pacific, sailing between the United States, Canada, Japan, China, Australia, and other nations.

PHYSICAL GEOGRAPHY

The Pacific Ocean Floor

Plateaus, peaks, plains, and trenches crinkle the Pacific Ocean floor. A shallow, narrow **continental shelf** borders the west coast of the Americas. Then a **continental slope** slants down to abyssal (deep-sea) hills and plains. Beyond these soars the East Pacific Rise, a huge submarine mountain chain cut across by cliffs at **transform faults**. West of these mountains lie more abyssal hills and plains. Then comes an area of mostly underwater peaks and plateaus, making the Pacific's western floor very rugged.

Like other ocean floors, the bed of the Pacific is part of Earth's **crust**. This consists of huge **plates**, locking together like

***Below:** A map of the rugged Pacific Ocean floor showing crustal plates (outlined in yellow) and groups of volcanic islands.*

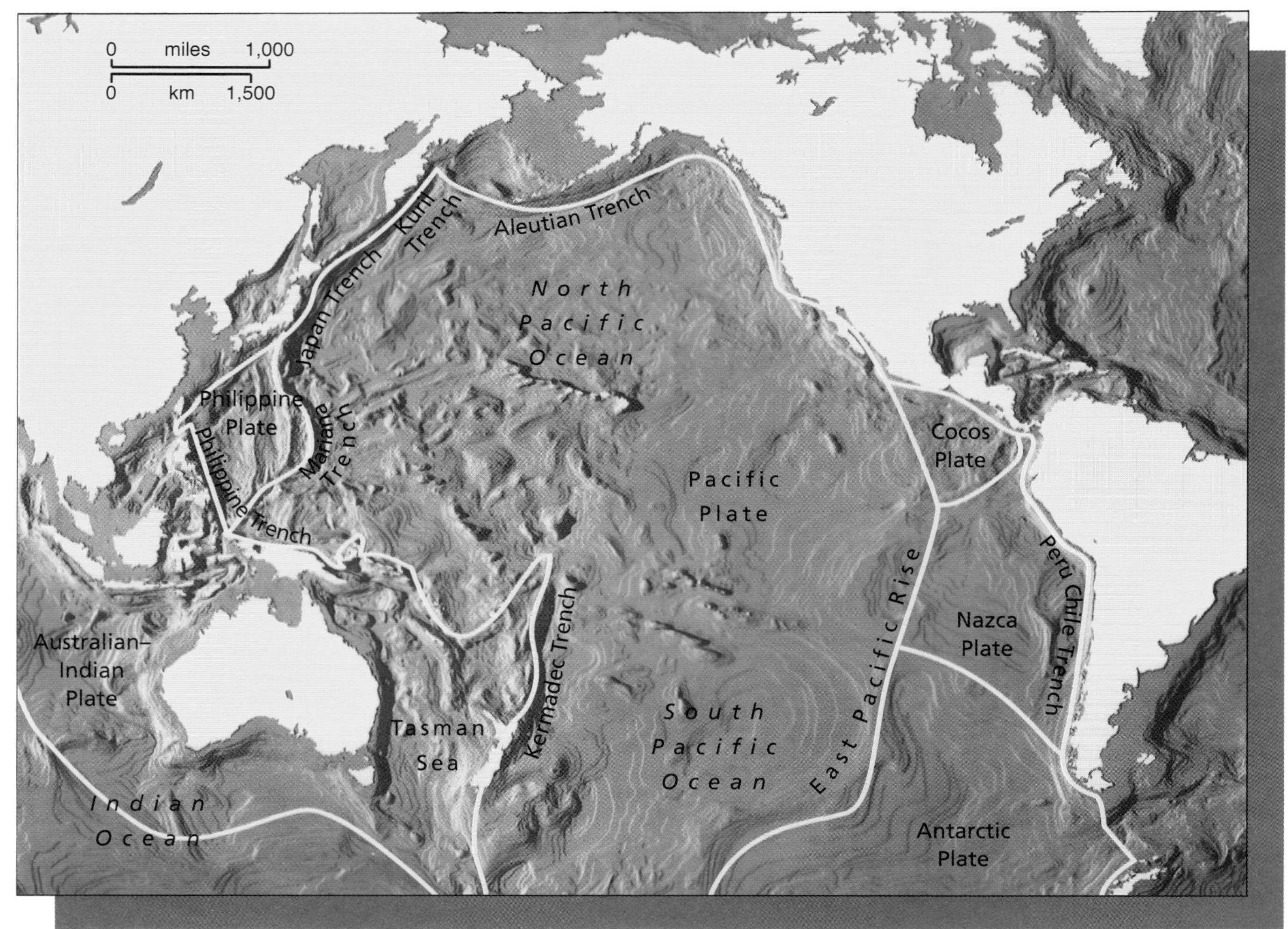

the pieces of a jigsaw puzzle. These plates float on Earth's **mantle**. The Pacific Plate is the largest oceanic plate on Earth. As it drifts slowly west toward Asia, a gap opens up between it and smaller oceanic plates to its east. To plug this gap, molten rock wells up from the mantle and builds a **spreading ridge**. Such rock created the East Pacific Rise. Molten rock once also punched holes up through the western half of the Pacific plate. Thick masses of **lava** poured out and piled up on the western Pacific floor, forming underwater plateaus and volcanic peaks.

Above: *A three-dimensional map of part of the East Pacific Rise, a spreading ridge west of South and Central America. It marks the boundary between the Pacific, Cocos, and Nazca plates.*

At the Pacific rim, slabs of oceanic crust dive under other slabs or beneath the lighter continental crust, thus forming some of the world's deepest trenches.

More ocean floor is being lost than made because the Pacific Ocean is shrinking, squeezed between the plates of Asia and Australia on one side and the Americas on the other. North America has already drifted west to overrun the northern end of the East Pacific Rise. In millions of years the Americas might eventually collide with Asia and Australia, breaking up the Pacific Ocean.

PHYSICAL GEOGRAPHY

Pacific Islands

Large West Pacific islands including Japan, New Guinea, and New Zealand once formed parts of nearby continents. Smaller islands are mostly the tops of volcanoes rising from the seabed. Hundreds of these **oceanic islands** are dotted around parts of the Pacific.

Curved rows of oceanic islands called island arcs occur around the Pacific's western and northern rims. The Japanese, Bonin, and Aleutian islands are such groups. Each of these island arcs appeared where a plate of oceanic crust, covered by **sediments**, slid deep down into the mantle beneath a plate of oceanic or continental crust and began to melt. This molten rock burned holes through the solid crust above, raising a row of volcanic islands made of **andesite** and **basalt** rock.

Far out in the Pacific stand lines of oceanic islands. These include the Hawaiian, Pitcairn-Tuamotu, and Tubai island chains. Each formed on an oceanic plate moving over a fixed hot spot in the mantle. Here, every million years or so, a plume of molten rock rises in the mantle and burns through the oceanic plate above, building a volcanic island made mostly of basalt rock. The slow-moving oceanic plate then

Above: *When these high volcanic islands in Tonga sink below the sea, their surrounding coral reefs will remain as low, narrow, ring-shaped islands called atolls.*

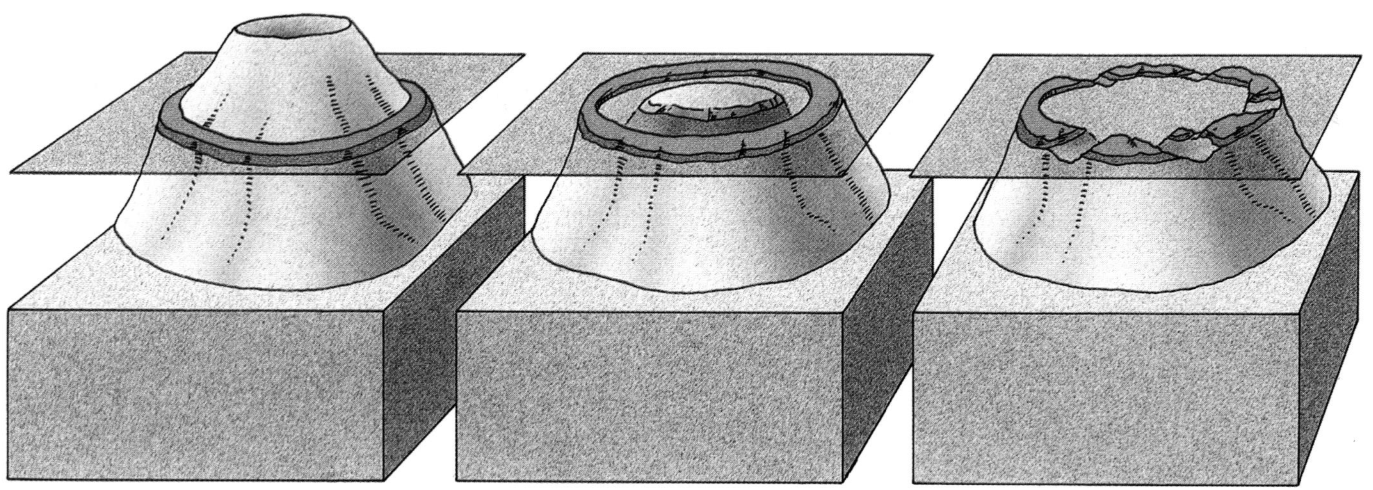

A fringing coral reef will grow in the shallow, clear water around a volcanic island.

The sea level rises or the volcano sinks, but the coral must grow toward the light, so it is always just above sea level.

The volcanic island is no longer visible and the coral reef remains, forming an atoll.

gradually carries this island away northwest, and another island sprouts over the same spot. This process has formed a line of islands, with the newest, highest island at the southeast end, closest to the hot spot.

Hundreds of old volcanic islands have disappeared—submerged as the sea level rose or the oceanic plate they stood on dipped. Meanwhile, tiny coral **polyps** built coral reefs in the clear, warm, shallow sea around many volcanic islands in the tropics. As each volcano sank, its reef kept growing up toward the light. When the island vanished, the reef remained as a low ring of coral islands called an atoll, encircling a pool of seawater called a lagoon. Most atolls occur in the Pacific. Kwajalein, the world's largest atoll, in the Marshall Islands, is about 190 miles in circumference.

***Below:** The Bay of Islands is part of North Island, one of New Zealand's two main land masses. Long ago, both of these land masses split off from a prehistoric supercontinent.*

PHYSICAL GEOGRAPHY

The Ring of Fire

The large number of active volcanic mountains earn the Pacific rim its nickname, the Ring of Fire. These mountains rose where slabs of oceanic crust were forced below slabs of continental crust. In Earth's hot interior, the sinking slabs warmed up and melted. Some of the lighter molten rock then flowed up through the continental crust to form volcanoes.

On the ocean's western side, volcanoes occur from New Zealand's North Island and north through the New Hebrides, Philippines, Japan, Kamchatka, the Kuril Islands, and the Aleutian Islands. On the eastern side of the Pacific, the volcanoes of North America's Cascade Range and South America's Andes form part of the mountain backbone running down the western side of the Americas. The Andes give their name to andesite rock.

Where Pacific coasts are low, there is usually a narrow strip of lowland with mountains inland. But in eastern China, the Huang and Yangtze, two of the world's largest rivers, have dumped mud that has built broad, low, fertile coastal plains.

Indochina, Korea, and Kamchatka jut out from mainland Asia, but the Americas' Pacific coast is straighter—Baja California is its only large **peninsula**. In southeast Alaska, western Canada, and southern Chile, however, the sea flooded valleys, forming inlets and a maze of islands.

Each year thousands of tiny earthquakes shake coasts of the Pacific rim as oceanic and continental plates collide. An earthquake relieves the pressure that builds up in the rocks when

***Above:** Smoke rises from the volcano Mayon in the Philippines.* Mayon *means beauty, and this volcano is often regarded as the most perfect cone-shaped volcano in the world. The black sand in front of the fishing village is volcanic material. Many more active volcanoes ring the Pacific.*

***Left:** Ruined, burned-out buildings still stand among the remains of others flattened by an earthquake. This was the Japanese city of Kobe in early 1995.*

one plate jams against another. Severe earthquakes happen when pressure has built up over many years. Then loss of life and damage can be huge. Hundreds of thousands of people died in Tangshan, China, in 1976. In 1995 Kobe suffered Japan's severest recorded earthquake—more than five thousand people died and much of western Kobe was destroyed. California, Taiwan, and Chile are other densely populated Pacific areas likely to suffer heavy earthquake damage.

Undersea earthquakes sometimes trigger giant tidal waves called tsunamis. A tsunami can travel thousands of miles and engulf low-lying shores.

PHYSICAL GEOGRAPHY

Climates, Currents, and Winds

Pacific climates range from hot in the tropics to cool in the far north and cold in the far south, but winds and currents cause local differences in climates.

El Niño

In some years, the Southeast Trade Wind fades out and stops pushing the cold Peru current north past Peru. It is replaced by a current of warm water flowing south from the Pacific Equatorial Countercurrent. Peruvians call this warm current El Niño ("The Child") because it usually arrives around Christmas, when they celebrate the anniversary of Jesus Christ's birth. El Niño itself is nothing to celebrate, for it kills or drives away the schools of fish that fishermen depend on and causes abnormal weather conditions. Sometimes so many fish die that their rotting bodies give off enough fumes to turn ships' paintwork black.

Flowing around the Pacific are two large systems of surface currents called gyres. The North Pacific Gyre flows clockwise. Its North Equatorial Current carries warm water westward north of the equator, then feeds the Kuroshio Current, bringing warmth north to Japan. The Kuroshio becomes the mild North Pacific Drift, which flows northeast away from the cold Kamchatka Current and heads south past Kamchatka. Off western North America, part of the North Pacific Drift turns north as the Alaska Current, which keeps Alaska's southern shores ice-free in winter. Another part turns south as the cool California Current, flowing past the United States before joining the North Equatorial Current to complete the North Pacific Gyre.

Water temperatures and salinity	
Pacific Ocean	
Surface temperature	28–90°F
Bottom temperature	30°F
Salinity (parts per thousand)	32–36.5

The South Pacific Gyre flows counterclockwise. Its South Equatorial Current flows west, south of the equator, then south past New Guinea and Australia as the East Australian Current. South of New Zealand this joins the chilly West Wind Drift, flowing east toward South America. To complete the South Pacific Gyre, the cold Peru, or Humboldt, Current flows north up the western coast of South America. Cold, dry winds that blow across this current keep much of coastal Chile and Peru dry and barren.

Between the North and South Pacific Gyres, the strong, warm Pacific Equatorial Countercurrent heads east, returning some of the water carried west by the equatorial currents on each side.

Four great belts of wind drive all these currents. In the far north and south, westerly winds push water east, and on each side of the Equator **trade winds** push the water west. But the fiercest winds blow around tropical rainstorms—especially the **typhoons** that track northwest toward the Philippines and China. Typhoons can snap palm trees, flatten buildings, and whip up waves that swamp low islands and even sink large modern ships.

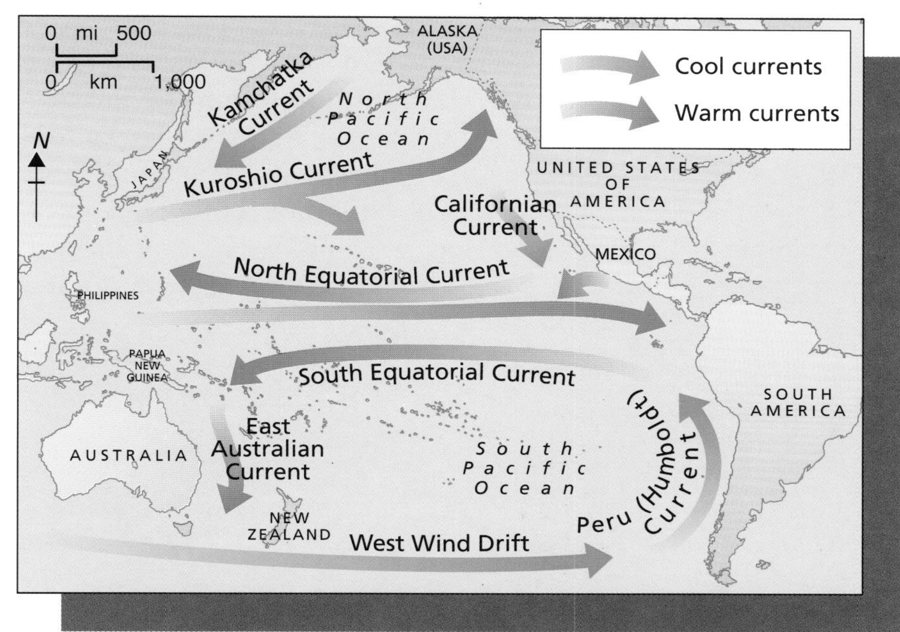

***Right:** Winds blowing toward the equator help steer the ocean currents circling the North and South Pacific. Warm currents are shown in red and cold currents are shown in blue.*

***Below:** A tropical typhoon over the western Pacific, photographed by the crew of the space shuttle* Discovery *in 1985. The shape of the typhoon and the eye of the storm at its center are clearly shown.*

Pacific Food Chains

As in every ecosystem, the Pacific's living things form **food chains**. In one food chain off Peru, phytoplankton (tiny, drifting water plants) are food for zooplankton (tiny animals that drift in surface waters). Schools of fish called anchoveta feed on the plankton. Anchoveta are preyed upon by bigger fish such as the Pacific bonito and yellowfin tuna as well as by brown pelicans, guanay cormorants, and other diving sea birds. Bonitos and yellowfins in turn fall prey to sharks and fishermen. The nutrients in this food chain get reused. Fish droppings, dead sea plants, and dead animals rain down on the ocean floor, providing food for scavenging **invertebrates**. Bacteria complete the cycle by breaking down seabed

***Below:** In this food chain the large fish—the bonitos and tuna—prey upon smaller fish—anchoveta—that feed on tiny zooplankton and phytoplankton.*

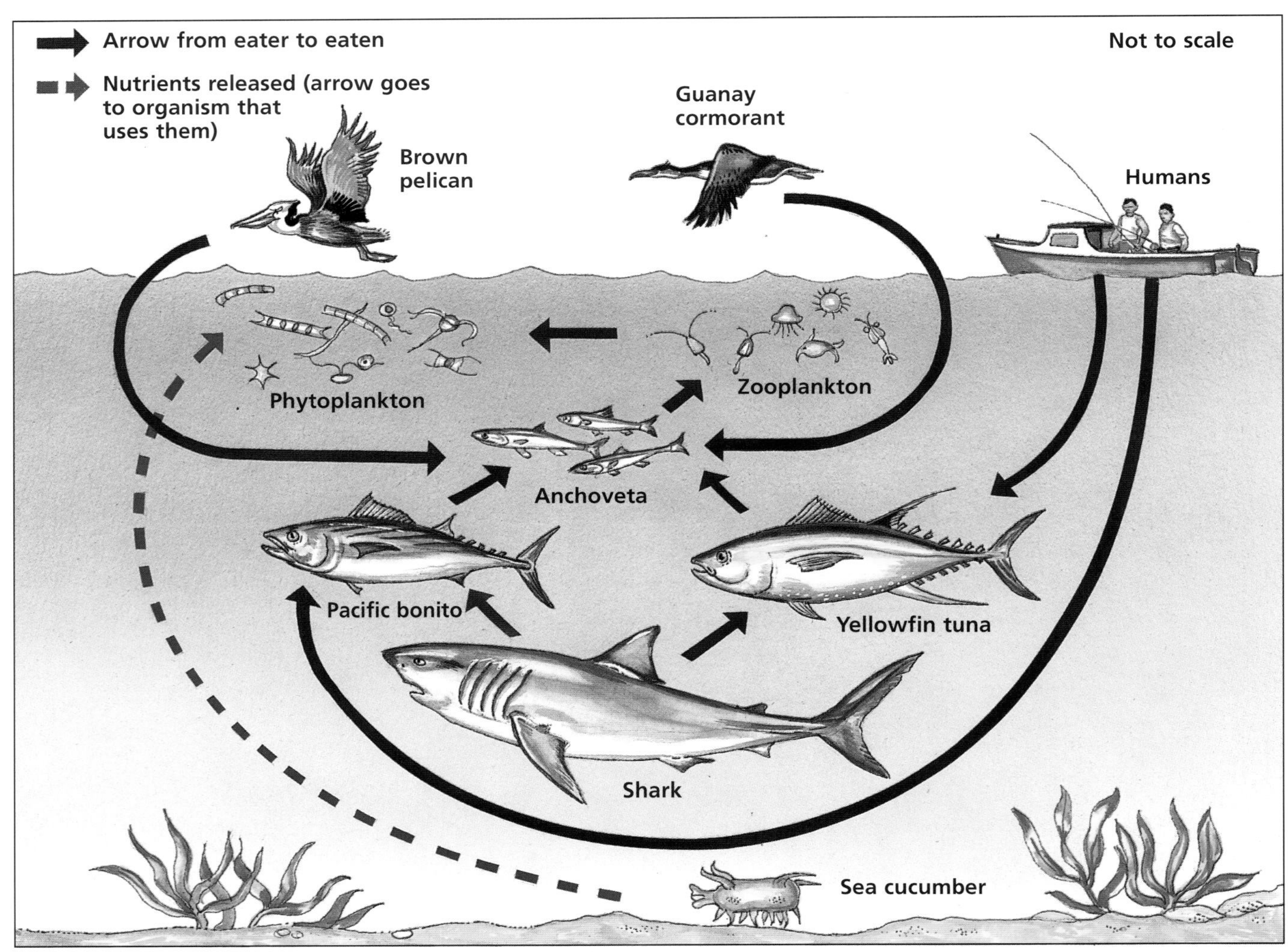

***Above:** Sunlight shines down through an underwater kelp forest off the coast of California. The seaweed provides many underwater animals with food and hiding places.*

droppings and dead organisms and releasing nutrients that the phytoplankton then use.

A food chain also forms a food pyramid, because a large number of one species forms one layer, which feeds fewer members of other species in the layer above, and so on. Billions of microscopic plants support millions of tiny animals, supporting thousands of small fish, supporting a few larger ones—enough to feed one shark or human being at the food pyramid's tip.

Food chains differ from one part of the Pacific to another, since the places plants and animals live depend on the water's temperature, depth, salinity (saltiness), and nutrients. For example, in cool coastal waters an important plant food is the Pacific giant **kelp**, the world's longest seaweed. The phytoplankton and seaweed that almost all Pacific animals depend upon live only in sunlit surface waters, and life is most plentiful where surface waters have the richest source of food. These places tend to lie where Pacific waters mix with cold Arctic and Antarctic waters and off Pacific coasts and islands. There, nutrient-rich water wells up from the ocean floor. But in much of the Pacific Ocean, far from land, few nutrients return to the surface, so life is much scarcer there.

OCEAN PLANTS AND ANIMALS

Marine Invertebrates and Fish

The Pacific's open ocean, wetlands, **mangrove** swamps, and coral reefs each has its own community of plants and animals. When people think of underwater life in the Pacific, coral reefs often come to mind. Northeast Australia's Great Barrier Reef is particularly well known. No fewer than three thousand species inhabit this reef's rocky surface or the shallow, warm, clear waters where it stands.

Around the Great Barrier Reef, life depends on reef-building coral polyps. Each polyp builds and hides inside a stony coral cup. At night it puts out stinging tentacles to capture food. By day, minute plants living in the polyp produce substances that the polyp needs. Because these plants need light, coral grows only near the surface, where it forms strange, brightly colored shapes that look like branches, brains, and platforms.

About two hundred kinds of coral occur in the Great Barrier Reef, providing food or shelter for creatures such as sea slugs, sea urchins, shrimp, crabs, giant clams, sea turtles, and 1,500 types of fish. Most reef fish are colorfully camouflaged or banded to make their outlines difficult to see against a reef background.

Animals living in Pacific Ocean coral reefs have close relatives in the Indian Ocean, because there is no land to keep tropical sea animals from traveling between the two oceans. Flying fish, tuna, and other warm-water fish of the open Pacific also have close relatives in the Atlantic Ocean, because before the isthmus of Panama joined North and South America, fish could swim freely between the

Strange Creatures

In 1977 scientists found strange animals living 1.5 miles below the surface of the eastern Pacific. Down there, on spreading ridges, it is pitch black and almost freezing. But molten volcanic rock heats seawater that passes underground. Full of dissolved minerals, the water boils and spurts up through holes called hydrothermal vents. Around these vents cluster giant tube worms, brown mussels, blind crabs, sea anemones, and other unusual creatures. All depend on microscopic bacteria, which manufacture food from the chemicals brought up by the underwater fountains. This discovery astonished scientists, because most animals depend on plants for food, and plants cannot make food without the help of sunlight.

Pacific and Atlantic. Now, however, the Americas and cold water to the north and south separate the warm-water fish of both oceans.

When two groups of the same species become separated, they **evolve** into different species over a long period of time. Breeding in separate rivers is perhaps the reason that the salmon of the North Pacific evolved into six species; but all of these are more closely related to each other than they are to the salmon of the North Atlantic.

Above: *Organ-pipe coral in the Solomon Islands. The polyps are open to catch plankton.*

Right: *Small fish swim above an underwater "garden" on Australia's Great Barrier Reef. Here, various kinds of living corals are shaped like cushions, plates, and shrubs.*

Pacific Reptiles, Birds, and Mammals

Most reptiles, birds, and mammals are land animals, but certain kinds have evolved for life in water. Some of these occur partly or only in the Pacific.

The Indo-Pacific crocodile—the world's largest reptile—haunts western Pacific coasts and islands from the Philippines to New Guinea and Australia and 1,500 miles farther east to Fiji. The western Pacific is also home to sea snakes, which never come ashore. Six species of sea turtles swim in warm Pacific waters. Among these is the leatherback, the world's largest living turtle.

Pacific sea mammals include whales, dolphins, sea otters, fur seals, sea lions, and sea cows. Sea otters and several kinds of fur seals and sea lions live only in the Pacific, and the *vaquita* (or Gulf porpoise), the world's smallest whale, lives only in the Gulf of California.

The coastal waters where whales and seals find food attract huge flocks of fishing seabirds. Large numbers of guanay cormorants and Peruvian boobies plunge into the ocean off Peru. Other species unique to the Pacific include several kinds of albatross, the Galápagos penguin, and the North Pacific's horned and tufted puffins.

Several Pacific creatures are long-distance migrants. Birds called slender-billed shearwaters circle the ocean, and gray whales swim thousands of miles between their Arctic feeding grounds and their breeding grounds in the Gulf of California.

***Above:** Galápagos fur seals were once hunted until there were very few left. They are now a protected species and their population is rising again.*

***Left:** A marine iguana warms up in the sun after plunging into the sea to browse on underwater seaweed. These lizards live only on the Galápagos Islands.*

Animals found nowhere else in the world inhabit isolated Pacific islands. New Zealand has two famous flightless birds, the kiwi and takahe. The strange lizardlike reptile, the tuatara, lives on small islands off New Zealand's coast. The Galápagos Islands west of Ecuador have even stranger beasts, including giant tortoises and marine iguanas—lizards that dive into the sea to feed on seaweed. These reptiles' ancestors drifted in from South America on floating islands of vegetation washed out to sea by rivers. Galápagos finches and Hawaiian honeycreepers, though, are descended from American birds storm-blown across the Pacific many thousands of years ago.

PEOPLING THE PACIFIC

Early Settlers

Most inhabited islands in the South Pacific region known as **Oceania** are chiefly occupied by one of three groups of people—Micronesians, Melanesians, or Polynesians.

Micronesians live in the Federated States of Micronesia, Kiribati and other island groups of Micronesia ("small islands") south of Japan and north of Melanesia. Melanesians live in Melanesia ("black islands")—the islands ranging from just north of New Guinea east to include Fiji. Some people consider New Guinea's **Papuans** to be Melanesians. Polynesians live scattered among the thousands of islands of Polynesia ("many islands")—an area inside a great triangle with its tips at Hawaii to the north, New Zealand five thousand miles to the southwest, and Easter Island four thousand miles to the east.

***Right:** This Micronesian girl lives on an island in the western Pacific just north of the equator. Once called the Caroline Islands, her homeland is now called the Federated States of Micronesia.*

Polynesians, Micronesians, and many Melanesians speak **Austronesian** languages, which can be traced back to the Chinese island of Taiwan. Their Austronesian-speaking ancestors were farmers and fishermen who sailed in canoes from southern China to Oceania about five thousand years ago. **Anthropologists** believe that these people settled among the people already living in Micronesia and Melanesia, and that the settlers populated the area by A.D. 1000. Papuans from New Guinea and Australian **aborigines** are descended from hunter-gatherers who arrived at least 60,000 years ago. They are thought to have come from Southeast Asia, probably walking most of the way. The sea level at that time was so low that only a narrow water gap separated Southeast Asia from a prehistoric continent containing New Guinea, Australia, and Tasmania.

While Southeast Asian peoples were settling the southern Pacific, Northeast Asian hunter-gatherers began crossing a prehistoric land bridge from Siberia to Alaska. By 10,000 years ago migrants from Asia had peopled the Americas from end to end. Their descendants today include the Inuitlike Aleuts of the Aleutian Islands, Native Americans of North America, and South America's Indians.

In this way, the first humans spread northeast and southeast from Asia to occupy the Pacific.

Below: *The three main groups of Pacific islands are called Micronesia, Melanesia, and Polynesia. Polynesia covers the largest area of the three.*

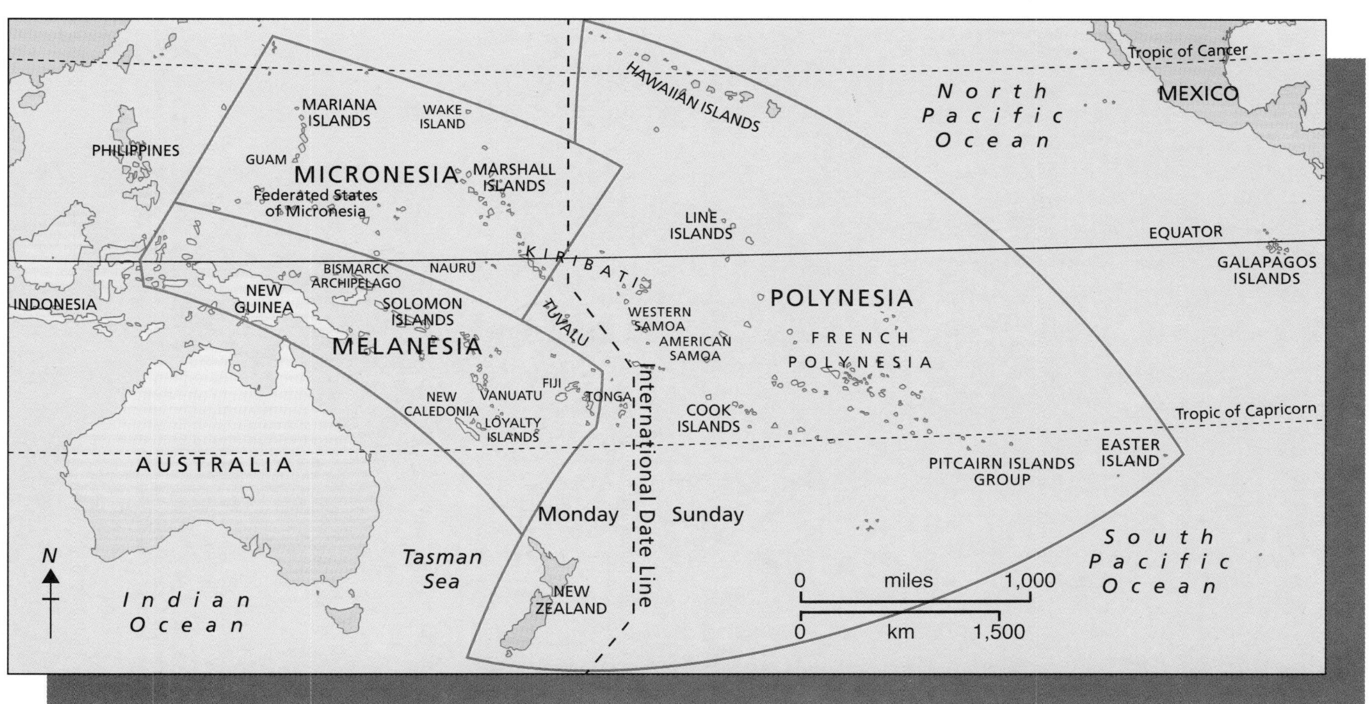

Western Impact on the Pacific

Pacific coasts and islands are still inhabited by the descendants of peoples who came from Asia thousands of years ago, but the Pacific region today is strongly influenced by the Europeans who appeared much later.

Easter Island

The impact of Europeans on Pacific peoples was nowhere harsher than on the Polynesians of Easter Island. In 1862 slave raiders took away one-third of the islanders to Peru to collect guano (seabird droppings used as fertilizer). Exposed to unfamiliar diseases and harsh conditions, most kidnaped islanders were dead within a year. Only 15 out of 1,000 returned. Unknowingly they brought back smallpox germs. Smallpox then killed all but 111 of the remaining 2,000 islanders. In 1888 the government of Chile forced the survivors into a small part of Easter Island and allowed a British company to raise sheep on the rest of the land.

Europeans first arrived in the Pacific region as explorers. In 1513 Spanish adventurer Vasco Núñez de Balboa crossed Central America and became the first European to see the Pacific Ocean. Portuguese **navigator** Ferdinand Magellan named the Pacific Ocean when he became the first European to sail across it between 1520 and 1521. In 1606 Dutchman Willem Jansz visited Australia, and in 1642 Dutchman Abel Tasman was the first European to reach New Zealand. Later explorers included Great Britain's Captain James Cook, who was the first European to reach New Caledonia, Hawaii, and other islands on voyages between 1768 and 1779 that crisscrossed the Pacific.

Trade followed exploration. Early on, European merchants wanted the spices that were grown in Southeast Asia. Later, traders collected coconut oil, sandalwood, and other Pacific island products. In colder regions, Russian fur traders visited Alaska, and ships of various nations hunted whales and fur seals in the far north and south.

After explorers and traders, European and American missionaries and settlers came. In the nineteenth century, settlers established coffee, sugarcane, and pineapple plantations in the tropics. By then, Europeans were laying claim to Pacific coasts and islands. Spain ruled the Philippines and much of the Americas until Spanish settlers formed their own nations.

Below: *Tourists enjoy the sun on Waikiki beach in Oahu, Hawaii. Today, Hawaii has a major tourist industry.*

Below: *Polynesians carved these giant stone heads on Easter Island in prehistoric times. Later, South America's European settlers arrived and made slaves of the islanders.*

Great Britain secured Australia, New Zealand, and Canada. The Dutch held what is now Indonesia and shared New Guinea with Germany and Great Britain. Russia occupied Siberia but sold Alaska to the United States. Hawaii and the Philippines came under U.S. control, and the United States, Great Britain, France, and Germany shared various other Pacific islands. By 1900 China and Japan were the only sizable Pacific nations still ruled by their original inhabitants, although the British held the Chinese island of Hong Kong.

These changes at first brought few benefits to the original Pacific peoples. Most had little say in government, many were forced to work under harsh conditions, and diseases spread by Europeans killed a large part of the population of certain islands.

PEOPLING THE PACIFIC

Pacific Peoples Since 1900

Great changes have affected Pacific island populations since 1900. In 1904 Japan became the first Asian nation to defeat a European power (Russia), and between 1931 and 1942 Japanese troops seized much of the Pacific's western and southern rim. U.S. and other Allied forces defeated Japan at the end of World War II in 1945 and handed back Japan's Pacific conquests to their prewar rulers. But then Pacific islanders began demanding self-rule. Australia and New Zealand had already become nations by 1907. Soon after World War II the Philippines and Indonesia gained independence. Between 1962 and 1991 so did much of Micronesia, Melanesia, and Polynesia. These areas became Western Samoa, Nauru, Fiji, Tonga, Papua New Guinea, the Solomon Islands, Tuvalu, Kiribati, Vanuatu, the Marshall Islands, and the Federated States of Micronesia. In the 1990s Western powers still held some Pacific islands. Hawaii had become the fiftieth of the United States in 1959, and the United States still governed part of Micronesia. France ruled French Polynesia and New Caledonia. Great Britain kept the Pitcairn Islands but agreed to hand Hong Kong back to China in 1999.

Meanwhile, Pacific lifestyles had been changing. Many islanders still lived in small fishing and farming villages, but in New Zealand, Australia, Hawaii, and Pacific Asian nations, millions flocked to modern cities. By the 1990s five of the world's largest cities stood on the Pacific rim. Old and new migrations meant that some Pacific islands gained mixed populations. Europeans, Japanese, Chinese, Filipinos, and Koreans far outnumber Polynesians in Hawaii. There are more Indians than Melanesian-Polynesians in Fiji, ten Europeans for every Polynesian Maori in New Zealand, and fewer than two in every hundred Australians is an aborigine.

Immigrants from Europe and Asia helped to more than double Oceania's population between 1950 and 1990. Yet 24 million of Oceania's roughly 27 million inhabitants live in Australia, New Guinea, and New Zealand. Some small island nations hold no more citizens than a small town. And while Oceania (including Australia) has nearly as much land as Europe, it contains less than one-fifth as many people.

Below:* *A village of thatched huts perches at the ocean's edge. Here in French Polynesia, many Pacific islanders still live as their ancestors did.

***Left:** Once, only Melanesian-Polynesians lived in Fiji. Now most Fijians are of mainly Indian origin.*

Shipping

Bathyscaphe *Trieste*

In 1960 the *Trieste* became the first manned vessel to visit a Pacific deep-sea trench. This bathyscaphe (*bathyscaphe* means "deep light boat") took two men to the lowest place on Earth—the floor of the Challenger Deep in the Mariana Trench. They sat in a hollow steel ball with windows thick enough to withstand over six tons of water pressure for every square inch. The ball hung from a big gasoline-filled float weighed down by 10 tons of iron pellets. The *Trieste* took five hours to reach the seabed about seven miles down. Its crew glimpsed living creatures. Then they began releasing iron pellets, and their bathyscaphe floated back up to the surface.

Despite its vast size, dangerous coral reefs, sudden storms, and pirates, the Pacific has been sailed for thousands of years. Chinese **junks** edged south to trade with Southeast Asia, and Polynesian canoes ventured far across the open ocean. Whole families migrated with their dogs, pigs, and food plants on **catamarans**, boats made by tying a platform across two canoes and adding a tall sail. Fishermen used outriggers (canoes supported by wooden floats stuck out to one side). Catamarans and outriggers could safely cross submerged coral reefs that would rip the bottom out of a boat with a deep **keel.**

Stone Age Pacific islanders became amazingly skillful navigators. Polynesians and Micronesians steered by the stars and found tiny atolls by following clues such as distant clouds, birds heading home to roost, and changes in the pattern of the waves.

***Left:** The bathyscaphe* Trieste*—a submersible research craft designed by Swiss professor Auguste Piccard and his son Jacques. The person standing on top gives us an idea of how big it was.*

***Above**: Many Pacific islanders still use traditional outrigger canoes. A float on each side balances this boat, which is carrying passengers along a coast in the Philippines.*

Most Pacific sea travel today is by large, fast vessels with modern navigation aids. Cargo goes in huge **bulk carriers**, **supertankers**, and **container ships**. Passengers island-hop by ferry or cruise liner or fly. Charts, radar, and **sonar** equipment help ships' captains avoid hitting reefs or atolls. Navigation satellites help pinpoint their positions, and weather satellites warn of approaching storms. In Southeast Asia, however, pirates are still a risk, boarding ships to steal cargo.

Special vessels and instruments explore the Pacific's lower depths. Deep-sea drills take samples from seabed rocks. Echo sounders map the Pacific floor by measuring its depth. Measurements involving Earth satellites show that the ocean crust is vanishing under the Kermadec-Tonga Trench faster than anywhere else.

Oceanographic research ships study deep-sea life. In 1951 the Danish vessel *Galathea* caught creatures nearly six miles down in the Philippine Trench, proving that life survives the tremendous water pressure at such depths. In the 1970s the tiny U.S. **submersible** *Alvin* actually filmed worms, clams, and other creatures on the Galápagos Rift, 1.5 miles deep.

Trade and Trade Routes

By the late twentieth century, four western Pacific places—Japan, Hong Kong, China, and South Korea—were among the world's ten largest owners of merchant vessels. Their cargo ships carried food, raw materials, and manufactured products across the Pacific and helped to make this one of the world's great ocean trading highways.

In the North Pacific huge quantities of goods travel between eastern Asia and North America, especially between Japan and the United States. But as much as one-third of all Pacific trade is among western Pacific nations, which together hold about one-third of all the people on our planet. Important western Pacific sea routes link Japan, Hong Kong, Southeast Asia, Australia, and New Zealand. In the eastern Pacific, goods go north and south by sea between ports on the west coast of the Americas.

Sea trade that reaches beyond the Pacific largely passes through two passages: at Singapore, where a narrow sea passage between Malaysia and Indonesia links the Pacific and Indian oceans; and at the Panama Canal, which cuts across Central America to link the Pacific with the Atlantic.

Below: *New Nissan cars wait on a Japanese dock for the ship that will take them abroad. By the 1980s Japan was selling large numbers of cars to the United States and Europe.*

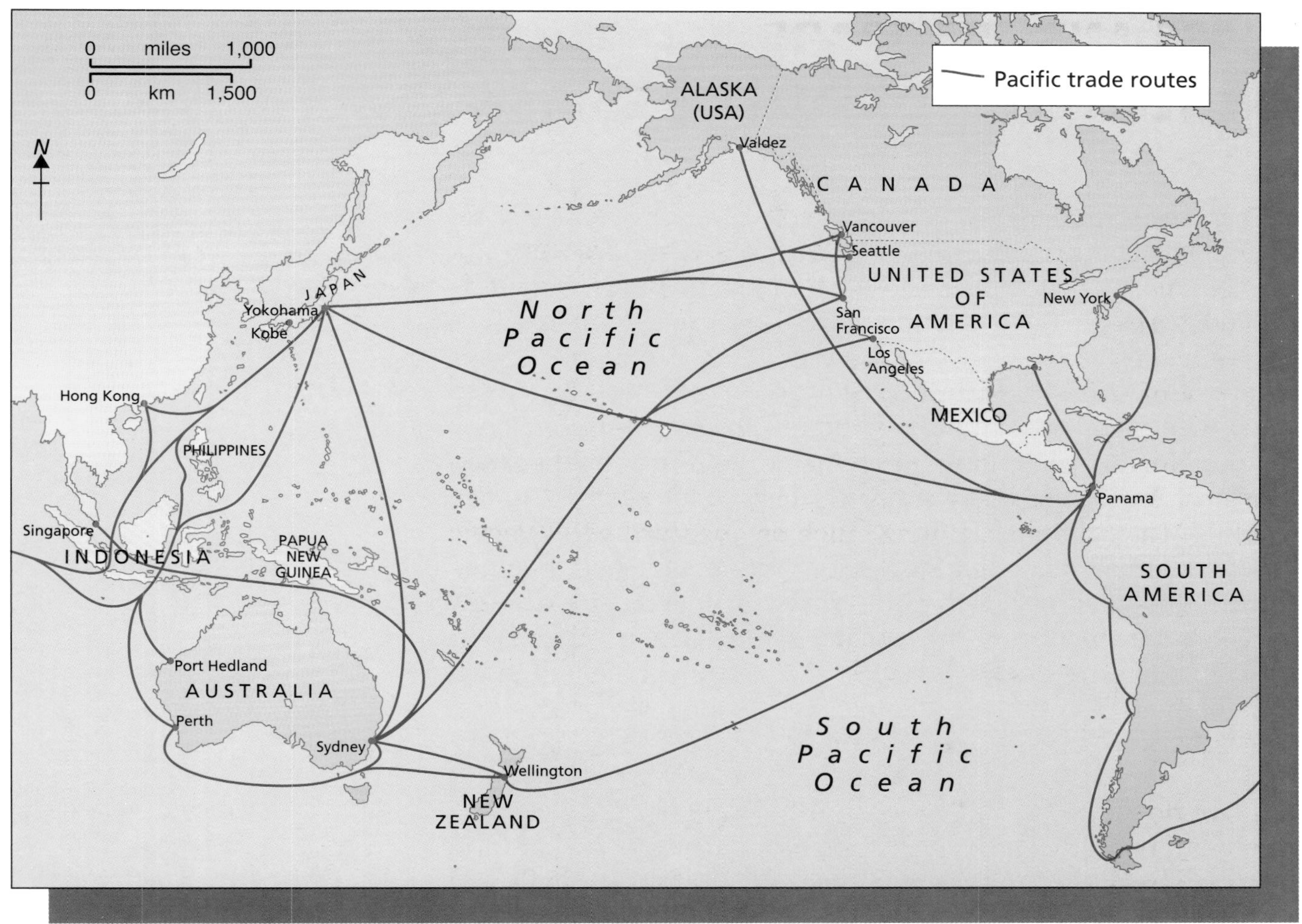

***Above:* This map shows the main trade routes crossing the Pacific Ocean and the chief ports that handle raw materials or manufactured goods.**

Much of the Pacific sea trade passes between some of the world's major ports. Among these are Singapore; Hong Kong; Yokohama and Kobe, Japan; Vancouver, Canada; Los Angeles, California; and Sydney, Australia.

Pacific ports handle cargoes of food and raw materials including cereals from Australia and western North America, hardwoods from Southeast Asia, oil from Southeast Asia and Alaska, and minerals from Australia, New Caledonia, and Chile. Most of these goods flow to west Pacific manufacturing nations, especially Japan. From Japan, China, Hong Kong, Taiwan, South Korea, and Singapore, ships carry cars, cameras, clothing, and other consumer products to countries around the world, but especially to the United States and Europe. By the late 1980s nearly two-fifths of Japan's goods went to the United States, and for the first time in American history U.S. trade with the western Pacific had become worth more than U.S. trade with Western Europe.

Mineral Resources

Parts of the Pacific Ocean or its coasts and islands are well supplied with minerals, **fossil fuels**, fish, forests, and fertile soil. By developing and using these resources, millions of Pacific people have become more prosperous than ever.

Minerals are particularly plentiful on or close to the Pacific rim, especially where molten rock has brought up substances such as copper, lead, and silver from deep in Earth's crust. Some of these elements have since been washed down to the ocean by rivers and dumped offshore with sands and gravels on the shallow seabed of the Pacific continental shelf. Patches of the shelf are covered with a crust of phosphates (useful fertilizers formed from the remains of dead sea creatures). In places, too, the rocks beneath the continental shelf have

Near-shore mineral resources
Chromite
Gas
Gold
Gravel
Iron
Monazite
Petroleum
Phosphorite
Sand
Tin
Titanium
Zircon

Deep-sea resources
Cobalt
Copper
Manganese
Nickel

Left: *An oil rig stands in shallow water off southeast Australia. Engineers now extract oil from rocks below the sea at several points of the Pacific rim.*

Above: *Bauxite being loaded onto a truck in a strip mine in the Northern Territory, Australia.*

trapped large quantities of oil and gas. Mines, dredging vessels, and drilling platforms extract these minerals and fossil fuels from land or sea.

Certain Pacific countries are particularly rich in mineral or fossil fuel resources. Australia mines more bauxite (used for making aluminum) than any other country and is a leading source of iron ore. Malaysia yields more than one-third of the world's tin. China is a major coal producer. China, Mexico, Alaska, and California pump up huge quantities of oil. California leads the United States for several minerals including boron (used for hardening steel), gravel, sand, and tungsten (used in electrical products). Peru and Mexico unearth more silver than any other countries. Chile is the world's second-largest copper-mining nation. Much of the world's nickel comes from New Caledonia and Indonesia.

On the other hand, Japan and many small Pacific island nations have hardly any minerals at all. Eventually, too, most land-based ores could be exhausted. Yet metallic lumps lie strewn thickly over the Pacific's bed, especially between Hawaii and Mexico. Deep-sea dredges towed by ships could mine these ocean-floor minerals.

Living Resources

Fish and shellfish rank high among the living resources of the Pacific region. At least half the world's total fish catch comes from the Pacific Ocean, mainly from its continental shelf. The North Pacific harvest includes salmon and fish that dwell on the seabed, such as pollack, cod, and bass. Inshore waters off Indonesia, Japan, California, and Peru produce sardines, mackerel, and other surface-swimming species. Tuna are often caught far out at sea. Japan's fish catch is the world's largest, and eight of the top ten fishing nations have Pacific coastlines.

Forests of the Pacific rim yield wood for making anything from paper to toothpicks and window frames. Useful trees include eucalyptus and conifers in Australia, tropical hardwoods in Southeast Asia, conifers in western North America, and southern beech in Chile.

There are large areas of land suitable for raising crops or livestock in New Zealand, Australia, Southeast Asia, and China, and belts of farmland run down the western coast of the Americas. Food crops range from wheat in northern China to rice, bananas, and yams in warm, rainy Southeast Asia. Cash crops (crops sold, not used by their growers) include citrus fruits and grapes in California and Chile; sugarcane in Australia, Hawaii, and the Philippines; pineapples in the Philippines, Mexico, and Hawaii; and coffee in Indonesia and Mexico.

Among the livestock raised on or close to the Pacific rim, sheep are very important in Australia, New Zealand, and the Andes Mountains. Australia exports more wool than any other country. Australia and Mexico produce cattle, and China is the world's chief pig producer.

Fish Farming

Farming captive fish is a surer way of getting food than hunting wild schools in the ocean. By the 1980s, each year Japan was raising 165,000 tons of yellowtail fish and smaller quantities of bluefin tuna in cages floating in the sea. Japanese fish farmers can increase a bluefin tuna's weight by 300 times in just four years. Japan also farms shellfish such as oysters and grows edible seaweed on fixed nets in the shallow waters of its inland sea, Seto-naikai. But China is the world's biggest fish-farming nation. As much as half the world's supply of farmed fish consists of freshwater species reared in Chinese ponds.

Above: *These brightly colored ribbons are really seaweed left out to dry. The Japanese grow seaweed as a valued source of food.*

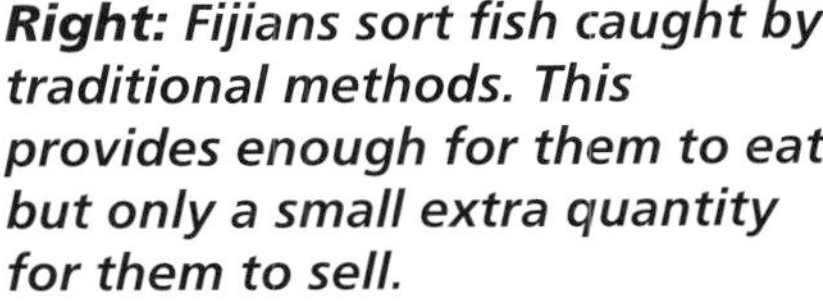

Right: *Fijians sort fish caught by traditional methods. This provides enough for them to eat but only a small extra quantity for them to sell.*

Out in the Pacific Ocean many atolls have too little rain or soil for cultivating crops or raising livestock. However, the moister tropical islands produce yams and coconuts. Copra (dried coconut flesh) is the chief product of the South Pacific islands. Its oil is used in soap and margarine.

RESOURCES OF THE PACIFIC REGION

Manufacturing

Parts of the Pacific rim make it the fastest-growing economic region in the world. This growth comes largely from factories.

Modern manufacturing in the Pacific region began in California. Since the 1960s California has earned more from manufacturing than any of the other states. Computers, electronic equipment, and aircraft are among its major products. But since World War II, production has also grown quickly on the other side of the Pacific.

Below: *An aerial view of Silicon Valley, California. Silicon Valley is famous for manufacturing computers and electronics.*

Right: *South Korean workers assemble cars in a Hyundai factory. South Korea is one of several Asian countries where manufacturing is growing quickly.*

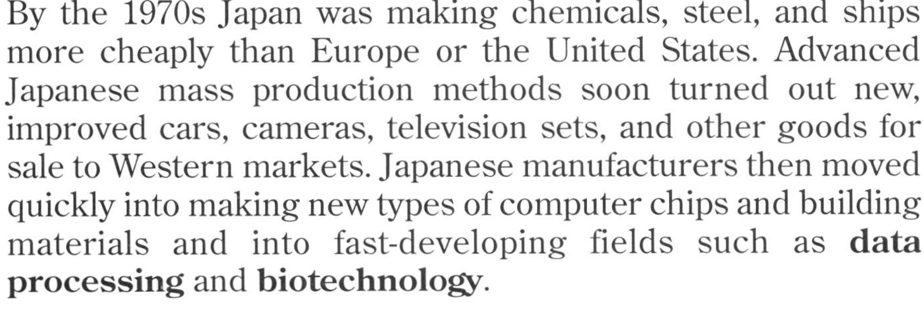

By the 1970s Japan was making chemicals, steel, and ships more cheaply than Europe or the United States. Advanced Japanese mass production methods soon turned out new, improved cars, cameras, television sets, and other goods for sale to Western markets. Japanese manufacturers then moved quickly into making new types of computer chips and building materials and into fast-developing fields such as **data processing** and **biotechnology**.

Japan's experience and money helped set up factories in nearby Asian countries. By the late 1980s, Hong Kong was the world's biggest manufacturing exporter of clothes, textiles, and toys. Taiwan had become well known for making aircraft parts, computers, and textiles. South Korea produced shoes, electronic equipment, cars, and more ships than any other nation. Singapore made data processing equipment and became a great trading and financial center, earning as much abroad as the huge nation of Australia. In most of these Asian countries, hardworking, low-paid workers made products that sold for much less than similar goods produced in North America or Europe, where factory workers earned far higher wages.

Asia's new industrial success spilled over into other countries in the region. By the 1990s Indonesia, Malaysia, Thailand, and the Philippines were fast building their own industries. Meanwhile China, with the world's largest population, encouraged foreign investors to help set up factories in special economic zones, and "open" cities that were designated for capitalist development. It is possible that in the twenty-first century China might even replace the United States as the greatest manufacturing nation in the world.

RESOURCES OF THE PACIFIC REGION

Tourism

One of the great natural resources of much of the Pacific region is its warm, sunny climate and tropical or subtropical scenery. Fast, long-distance flights bring tourists by the millions to enjoy vacations on silvery, palm-fringed beaches lapped by a clear ocean. Extra attractions are often the traditional clothes and customs of local peoples.

__Right:__ Two sea lions bask in the sun, unconcerned with a boatload of people exploring the Galápagos Islands.

Each year, many tourists head for beach resorts in Bali, Indonesia; Acapulco, Mexico; Honolulu, Hawaii; and the Gold Coast, Australia. Visitors also flock to Pacific cities such as Singapore; Hong Kong; Vancouver, Canada; San Francisco, California; and Sydney, Australia. Increasing numbers take special-interest vacations. For example, sport fishing enthusiasts hunt marlin in the Gulf of California in Mexico, and natural history enthusiasts visit coral reefs or watch whales off coasts as far apart as Alaska and New Zealand.

To serve their visitors, Pacific countries have built or enlarged airports, hotels, restaurants, and sports facilities. All these provide work for the people living there. In places like Hawaii, tourism contributes enormously to the economy.

__Below:__ Maoris demonstrate a war dance for tourists visiting New Zealand.

Yet remote Pacific islands and mountainous or desert parts of the Pacific rim are rarely visited. In such places some isolated peoples live in ways that have hardly changed for centuries. Some islanders still grow their own food and make their own clothing.

Where there is no tourism, trade, or manufacturing to increase earnings, incomes are extremely low. This means there are huge differences in living standards throughout the region.

In economically developed California, Japan, and Australia, people are far better off than those in rural China, Indonesia, Peru, and most small oceanic islands. In 1990 the average Indonesian's yearly income was only about $500—less than one-thirtieth the average income in Japan and less than one-fortieth the average income in the United States. China's average income was even lower than Indonesia's. In both these countries, though, earnings should increase as cities prosper.

EFFECTS ON THE ENVIRONMENT

Environmental Problems

As Pacific populations grow, their increasing needs for food, raw materials, and living space are having damaging effects on coasts, islands, and offshore waters.

Cities of the Pacific rim have expanded to cover great areas in roads and buildings. Tokyo and Hong Kong have even created airports on land made by dumping rubble into the sea. Vast quarries demolish mountains in western Australia and tropical forest in New Caledonia and New Guinea. Quarrying has even stripped coral reefs and sands from stretches of Pacific coast. In the Philippines, workers broke up and carried off whole reefs for use as building materials. In Bali, storm waves gnawed away at low shores left unprotected where offshore coral reefs have been removed.

Meanwhile, logging is destroying forests. The tropical hardwood forests of Malaysia, Indonesia, and the Philippines are felled to produce wood for east Asian factories and land for local farmers. Even where logging takes only the largest trees, it damages most of the remaining ones. Much of the tropical rain forest that once covered most of Southeast Asia is gone. The rest could soon disappear along with its native wildlife, including thousands of undiscovered species. **Clear-cutting** also threatens ancient Australian hardwood forests and coniferous forests on the Pacific coast of northwest North America. Even the tropical mangrove swamp forests have been vanishing. For years Indonesia annually turned more than 900 square miles of coastal mangroves into wood chips. Fish and shellfish living in the mangrove swamps lost their feeding grounds and died.

Exxon Valdez

One of the worst oil spills anywhere happened in the North Pacific in 1989. The supertanker *Exxon Valdez* ran aground in Prince William Sound off southern Alaska, leaking 11 million gallons of crude oil. Within a week the oil spread more than one thousand square miles. Washed along by currents, the slick coated rocks and beaches in a sticky blanket that smothered much of Alaska's southwest coast. The oil poisoned or suffocated huge numbers of fish, seabirds, and sea mammals, including sea otters and sea lions. Some conservationists believe more than 1,000 sea otters and 100,000 seabirds died.

Left: *Seen from the air, reddish-orange oil pollutes a rocky Alaskan shore. This was just a little of the oil spilled when the* Exxon Valdez *ran aground in 1989.*

Below: *Mud smothers and kills corals on this part of Australia's Great Barrier Reef. The main cause is careless farming, which lets soil wash into the sea.*

Removing coral reefs and forests wipes out wildlife altogether, but marine wildlife also suffers from pollution. This is mainly caused by human sewage, chemicals from factories and ships, **pesticides** and fertilizers, and soil left bare on hillsides and then washed away by rain. Sewage killed almost all the corals at one end of Kameohe Bay off the Hawaiian island of Oahu. In Australia and Hawaii, millions of tons of soil smothered and killed coral reefs and their inhabitants. By the 1970s Japanese waters were experiencing more than two thousand pollution incidents each year.

Where reefs are damaged, fewer fish remain for fishermen to catch. This makes a bad situation worse, for **overfishing** is reducing the Pacific Ocean's fish stocks. By the 1990s huge Asian, Russian, and eastern European fishing fleets were catching Pacific fish faster than these species could breed to replace the numbers caught. In particular, numbers of anchovies, halibut, king crabs, Pacific Ocean perch, and Pacific salmon had become far scarcer than they had been. Heavy fishing not only affects fish stocks—other damage can also result. Tens of thousands of small whales, sea lions, turtles, seabirds, and other accidental victims die every year in drift nets up to 25 miles long.

Overcollecting is another danger. Pacific islanders sell quantities of coral and seashells taken from the reefs to tourists. Indonesians kill up to 50,000 marine turtles a year, largely to sell their shells as tourist souvenirs. No wonder turtles, corals, and seashells are becoming rare in parts of the Pacific.

Special problems arise where countries have dumped nuclear waste or tested nuclear bombs in or near the Pacific Ocean. Until the 1980s American planes and barges regularly dropped containers of radioactive waste in Pacific coastal waters. Radioactivity from leaking containers could

__Below:__ Although entangled by a fishnet, this northern fur seal survived to swim ashore on Russia's Komandorskie Islands. Many other seals and sea lions are less lucky.

Above: *A mushroom cloud rises following the explosion of an 11-megaton nuclear bomb at Bikini Atoll in the 1950s.*

make it dangerous to eat fish from these areas. By 1958 the United States had exploded 70 nuclear bombs on Bikini and Eniwetok in Micronesia, and by 1995 France had detonated more than 80 on Mururoa in French Polynesia. Some of the nuclear explosions released enough radioactivity to harm local wildlife, and the huge explosions made Mururoa atoll start to sink.

EFFECTS ON THE ENVIRONMENT

Problems For People

Damage done to the Pacific environment is also likely to harm local peoples. Pollution has caused sickness and death. By 1983 more than six hundred Japanese villagers had died from eating shellfish that had been poisoned by mercury, which was dumped by a factory near Minamata Bay. By 1990 nuclear bomb testing had driven some Micronesians and Polynesians from their homes and caused fatal cancers. In 1995 France resumed nuclear testing on Mururoa despite worldwide criticism. The full effects may not be seen for many years.

Where Pacific peoples use resources faster than nature replaces them, food shortages or hunger could result. When tropical forests are cleared, new large trees might never grow. If soil is washed away from deforested hillsides, there is nothing to support trees or crops, so forest peoples lose their way of life. Where coral reefs and mangrove swamps have disappeared, local people lose valuable fishing grounds. Where foreign fishing fleets seize all the tuna, island nations are robbed of a major food supply.

Below: *This atoll and other islands of the small low-lying Pacific nation of Kiribati could all be drowned if melting ice sheets at the poles raise the level of the ocean.*

***Right:** Beautiful tropical coral and sea creatures are displayed for tourists after a cruise around Fiji. But the overcollection of this sea life destroys the local environment.*

As overfishing depletes fish stocks, fishermen lose work. That has already happened in Peru and Mexico. Where overcollecting kills off turtles, coral, and seashells, islands might become less attractive to visit. If tourist numbers drop, local people lose a valuable source of income.

Sometimes fishermen's and other people's interests clash. In the mid-1990s, Ecuador's government banned the overcollecting of edible sea cucumbers off the Galápagos Islands. As a result, angry fishermen threatened to kill the islands' giant tortoises—the rarities that attract most tourists.

Countries that burn coal, oil, and gas may be causing a rise in temperatures worldwide and thawing polar ice sheets. This is known as global warming. Already, melting ice is thought by some scientists to be raising the level of the sea. By the year 2050 the oceans could have risen 20 inches. The rising sea would submerge low-lying farmland, depriving Pacific islanders of crops. Whole groups of atolls could drown, among them most of Kiribati, Tokelau, and Tuvalu. Thousands of Pacific islanders would lose not just their homes, but their nations.

Repairing Environmental Damage

Most people now realize that Pacific fish, coral reefs, coasts, and forests supply food and other resources too precious to be lost.

Conservationists and others work to remove pollution and prevent long-term disasters. After the *Exxon Valdez* oil spill, the oil company responsible paid teams to try to wash and scrape oil off Alaskan shores. To stop France from exploding test bombs on Mururoa, members of the conservation group Greenpeace protested. When trawlers threatened to overfish an area of sea, local Indonesian fishermen attacked the trawlers' crews. In Malaysia and Tasmania, public opinion prevented development from destroying important forests. In the United States, factories stopped canning tuna caught in drift nets because these also catch and kill animals such as dolphins. In Queensland, Australia, farmers, sewage-plant operators, and road builders are changing their ways of working so that soil and sewage no longer pour into the sea and kill coral reefs.

***Right:** Off Australia's Queensland coast, the Greenpeace sailing ship* **Red Bill** *campaigns to make a turtle breeding area a protected nature park.*

***Below:** A tug tows a floating oil boom into place. After the* **Exxon Valdez** *disaster, such booms stopped some of the spilled oil from spreading even farther than it did.*

Pacific governments protect their nations' offshore fishing grounds from being overfished by their own and foreign fishermen. Japan, Ecuador, and Indonesia also encourage fish or shrimp farming to make up for disappearing fish stocks.

International organizations work with governments to protect endangered resources. The United Nations Regional Mangrove Project has more than a dozen Asian and Pacific countries now trying to preserve mangrove forests. More than 60 countries, many in the Pacific area, have declared hundreds of coral reefs special protected areas. In the mid-1990s, 26 Pacific nations launched a campaign to save marine turtles from being hunted to extinction.

Unfortunately, environmental protection is only partly successful. Poachers illegally kill protected Pacific animals. An international timber growers' and users' plan for conserving tropical forests might have the opposite effect. New governments could throw out laws protecting reefs or forests. Global warming might become unstoppable. The Pacific environment will not be safe while human needs and numbers grow and while people fail to act responsibly.

Glossary

Aborigines The first or earliest known inhabitants of a place.
Andesite The brown or grayish rock that makes up some Pacific rim volcanoes.
Anthropologists People who study the societies and structures of mankind.
Austronesian A group of languages spoken in most of Southeast Asia and the South Pacific.
Basalt A dark, volcanic rock that wells up at spreading ridges and forms oceanic crust.
Biotechnology Using biological knowledge for industrial purposes.
Bulk carriers Big cargo ships designed to carry large, loose loads such as iron ore.
Catamarans Boats with two hulls side by side.
Clear-cutting Chopping down trees to clear a large area.
Container ships Cargo ships that carry goods prepacked in large, standard-size containers.
Continental shelf The submerged edge of a continent that slopes gently to a depth of about 600 feet.
Continental slope The slope leading down beyond the edge of a continental shelf.
Coral reefs Large, rocky structures built by the growth of tiny living coral polyps over many years.
Crust The hard, rocky surface of Earth.
Data processing Organizing information using computers.
Evolve To change gradually.
Food chains Chains of plants and animals, in which each species is dependent on the previous one in the chain for food.
Fossil fuels Natural fuels such as coal, gas, and oil, which were formed millions of years ago from the remains of living plants and animals.
Invertebrates Animals without backbones, such as snails.
Junks Wooden ships with high sterns, flat bows, and square sails made of cloth or matting.
Keel The beam that juts out along the bottom of a ship and supports the ship's structure.
Kelp A type of large brown seaweed.
Lava Molten rock that comes from volcanoes.
Mangrove A tropical tree or shrub rooted in shallow water on a low, muddy coast.
Mantle The layer of hot rock that lies below Earth's crust.
Navigator A person who guides a ship to its destination, avoiding dangers and obstacles along the route.
Oceania The collective name for the islands of the central and southern Pacific Ocean.
Oceanic islands Islands formed by volcanoes rising from the sea.
Overfishing Catching fish faster than those that are left can breed to replace them.
Papuan A native of New Guinea.
Peninsula A piece of land that juts out into a sea or ocean and is surrounded by water on three sides.
Pesticides Chemicals used to control animal pests.
Plates Enormous slabs of rock that form Earth's crust.
Polyps Small, cylindrical sea animals that attach to larger bodies. Over thousands of years the skeletons of coral polyps form coral reefs.
Sediments Sand, silt, mud, or other substances that have settled on the beds of lakes, rivers, or seas.
Sonar Short for SOund NAvigation Ranging. Sonar devices use sound waves and supersonic waves to find underwater objects.
Spreading ridge An undersea mountain ridge formed by molten rock rising from the mantle to plug the gap where two crustal plates have moved apart.
Submersible A small diving vessel, usually for two or three people, mainly for scientific or engineering jobs in deep water.
Supertankers Very large ships for transporting liquid cargo.
Trade winds Winds that blow steadily from the subtropics toward the equator.
Transform faults Cracks in Earth's plates where one plate jerks sideways against another. Transform faults cut across spreading ridges.
Typhoons Fierce tropical storms in the China Sea, off the Philippines, or in other areas of the Pacific.

Further Information

FURTHER READING

Baines, John D. *Protecting the Oceans*. Conserving Our World. Milwaukee: Raintree Steck-Vaughn, 1990.
Baker, Lucy. *Life in the Oceans*. New York: Scholastic, Inc., 1993.
Brooks, Felicity. *Seas and Oceans*. Understanding Geography. Tulsa: EDC, 1994.
Lambert, David. *Seas and Oceans*. New View. Milwaukee: Raintree Steck-Vaughn, 1994.
Macdonald, Robert. *Islands of the Pacific Rim and Their People*. People and Places. New York: Thomson Learning, 1994.
Sargent, William. *Night Reef: Dusk to Dawn on a Coral Reef.* New England Aquarium Books. New York: Franklin Watts, 1991.
Talen, Maria. *Ocean Pollution*. Overview. San Diego: Lucent Books, 1994.

FOR OLDER READERS:

Middleton, Nick. *Atlas of the Natural World*. World Contemporary Issues. New York: Facts on File, 1991.
The Pacific Ocean. World Nature Encyclopedia. Milwaukee: Raintree Steck-Vaughn, 1988.
Theroux, Paul, *The Happy Isles of Oceania: Paddling the Pacific*. New York: Putnam, 1992.

CD-ROM

Geopedia: The Multimedia Geography CD-Rom. Chicago: Encyclopedia Britannica.

USEFUL ADDRESSES:

Australian Conservation Foundation, 6726 Glenferrie Road, Hawthorn, Victoria 3122, Australia

Center for Environmental Education, Center for Marine Conservation, 1725 De Sales Street NW, Suite 500, Washington, DC 20036

Earthwatch Headquarters, 680 Mount Auburn Street, P.O. Box 403, Watertown, MA 02272-9104

Index

DATE DUE	BORROWER'S NAME	ROOM NUMBER

551.46 LAM
Lambert, David.
The Pacific Ocean